Origin

# What Do Bugs Eat?

Haydn Middleton

## Contents

**OXFORD**
UNIVERSITY PRESS

# Bug food

What does a bug eat and drink?

Does it eat and drink the same things as you?

# Spider

fly

spider

This spider has got a fly in its web.

The spider will eat the fly.

# Ladybird

This ladybird has found some aphids. Ladybirds eat aphids.

aphids

ladybird

Aphids on a plant.

Aphids need food too. They drink the sap from plants.

# Flea

flea

cat

This cat has fleas on its fur.
The fleas will bite the cat.
Then they drink its blood.

Fleas can jump on to you.
Then they drink *your* blood.

# Water bear

A water bear is a very small bug. It is smaller than the dot on this letter i.

water bears

What does something that small eat? Something even smaller!

# Dung beetle

This is a dung beetle. Do you know what it eats?

dung

dung beetle

It eats dung! It rolls dung into a ball with its legs.

# Ant

Ants are small bugs. They can eat much bigger bugs. Ants hunt for food in a team.

locust

ants

A team of ants can catch and eat a much bigger bug!

# Whose food?

Look at these bugs. Can you remember who eats who?

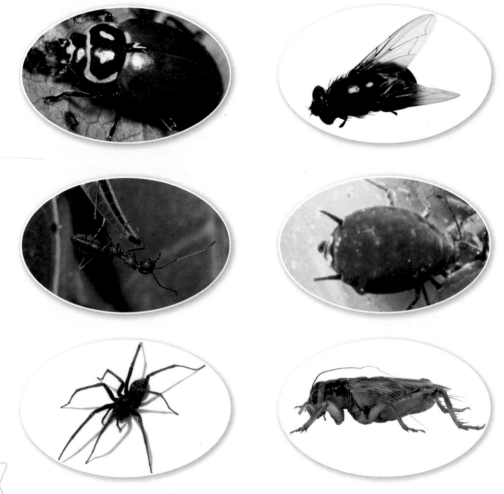